A LOO WITH A VIEW

A LOO WITH A VIEW

Luke Barclay

Published by Virgin Books 2008

2 4 6 8 10 9 7 5 3 1

Copyright © Luke Barclay 2008

Luke Barclay has asserted his right under the Copyright, Designs and Patents Act 1988 to be
identified as the author of this work

Designed by Words & Pictures Limited, London

First published in Great Britain and the United States of America in 2008 by Virgin Books
Random House, 20 Vauxhall Bridge Road, London SW1V 2SA

www.virginbooks.com
www.rbooks.co.uk

Distributed in the USA by Macmillan

Addresses for companies within The Random House Group Limited can be found at:
www.randomhouse.co.uk/offices.htm

The Random House Group Limited Reg. No. 954009

A CIP catalogue record for this book is available from the British Library

UK ISBN 9781905264230

USA ISBN 9781905264483

The Random House Group Limited supports The Forest Stewardship Council [FSC], the leading
international forest certification organisation. All our titles that are printed on Greenpeace
approved FSC certified paper carry the FSC logo.

Our paper procurement policy can be found at www.rbooks.co.uk/environment

Printed and bound by Firmengruppe APPL, aprinta druck, Wemding, Germany

For Mary

Contents

Introduction

Many years ago, on a family holiday, I found myself sitting on a loo in the upstairs bathroom of a Cornish cottage. As I sat doing my thing, a well-placed window offered views of an ancient chapel in a field on the cliff top. It was my first ever experience of a loo with a view – an exhilarating, heart-pounding, life-changing moment.

Two years ago, while sitting on another loo (which only had a view of a bath) I made a promise to myself. My mission was simple. I would seek out and document the world's best loos with views. It has been quite a journey. Considering the amount of loitering I have done in toilets with a camera, it is a miracle that I'm not in prison.

When I set out on my quest, I thought I was alone. But along the way I have met other loo-with-a-view enthusiasts from all over the world – many of their wonderful photographs appear in this book. Together, we form a small but enthusiastic global community –

undivided by class, race or religion – united by a love of loos that have views.

According to the World Toilet Organisation (there really is one), we spend around three years of our lives in the toilet. That is a long time to be sitting and staring at a door. Answering the call of nature should be uplifting and entertaining, thought-provoking and enlightening. It can be.

It has been well documented that as Buzz Aldrin descended the ladder of the lunar module, he stopped, paused and, with millions watching, started to fill the 'pee bag' in his spacesuit. The second man to walk on the moon had just become the first man to pee on it – boldly 'going' where no man had 'gone' before.

Luckily, we don't need to travel to the moon to enjoy a loo with a view. From open-air loos in National Parks, to urinals in front of windows, to compost toilets on tropical islands, to toilet blocks on the summits of sacred mountains, there are plenty of great examples here on Earth.

THE LOOS

Boulder Pass Campsite

Glacier National Park, Montana, United States

View: the world at its most beautiful and most fragile

You sit enthroned – exposed, alone and exhilarated – at one with nature. For loo-view purists this is what it is all about. No protection, no sinks, no soap dispensers. It is just you, a loo and a spectacular view.

The loo (photographed with the lid down), is known as a 'low rider' – a simple wooden box with a seat, designed to sit on ground in which it is difficult to dig a pit. And there is certainly plenty to keep your mind occupied whilst using it – as you look out at the Agassiz Glacier; it is frightening to think that in 1850 the glacier covered some four square kilometres, but by 1993 had shrunk to just one.

Open-air toilets offer some of the most exhilarating and thought-provoking loo experiences on the planet. They are out there waiting to be used and enjoyed. So get out of your bathroom, get into the wild (taking all appropriate precautions) and go find yourself a low rider.

Mount Fuji

Central Honshū, Japan

View: unforgettable toileting – see Japan awake beneath you from the summit loo

They climb through the night in their thousands to see the sun rise over the land of the rising sun. And waiting on the summit at over 12,000 feet is a post office, a restaurant, vending machines selling hot coffee and, of course, state-of-the-art toilets.

This is a spotlessly clean, fully flushable, unisex facility. And with each cubicle boasting its own window, it is a loo with a view that everyone can enjoy.

Incredibly, reports suggest that atmospheric music from the restaurant can sometimes be heard from the stalls – creating one of the world's great loo experiences. As English tourist Sam Jones explained: 'I stood at the urinal looking at a silhouetted Shinto shrine, while listening to Aerosmith's "I Don't Wanna Miss a Thing" – it was awesome!'

Visiting Fuji is a pilgrimage for the Japanese. There are numerous toilets on the mountain to serve the 200,000 or so who climb each year. The price of using one rises with altitude, peaking at 200 yen. A brave band of attendants live on the mountain to maintain standards.

N Seoul Tower

Seoul, South Korea

View: good for the 'Seoul' – stand and see a city beneath your feet

The urinals in Seoul Tower's 'Sky Restrooms' are purpose-built loos with views – part of a new wave that is reinventing the indoor toilet experience. All too often dank, windowless and depressing, this is the way it ought to be.

They offer a near picture-perfect view of the South Korean capital. For those who step up to the plate it is an unforgettable, uplifting and reaffirming experience. 'I feel ten feet tall,' said one user. 'I'm back,' said another.

Seoul Tower stands proud on top of Mount Namsan. It was refurbished and reopened in 2005 and branded as the 'N Seoul Tower'. The N stands for both 'new' and 'Namsan'.

Reports suggest that the 'Sky Restrooms' are advertised in the tower's elevator. It is a happy day when a toilet becomes a tourist attraction in its own right.

The ladies' restroom also has a view – from the sinks. Now that is a great hand wash.

Cliff-Top Chateau

The Dordogne, France

View: contemplate your future above a bend in the Dordogne River

The humble toilet is a sanctuary – an island of calm in a sea of stress. Away from the pressures of the world, it is the perfect place to escape and find distance, the perfect place to sit and ponder.

And located in a cliff-top French chateau with a view of one of the world's most picturesque rivers, this WC is, arguably, the most relaxing and thought-provoking toilet on Earth. When it comes to philosophising on the loo it does not get any better than this.

Rivers have long been seen as a metaphor for life. They have a beginning and an end. They are filled with twists and turns, as well as hidden dangers (e.g. anacondas). They can flow quickly or slowly, you can try to steer a course or allow yourself to go with the flow. But whatever happens, a river will keep on flowing (except during a severe drought) and you never know what's around the next bend.

The bathroom has recently been renovated and the position of the toilet reversed, no doubt to counter the neck-ache caused by years of looking left.

As well as providing an insight into the nature of life, the Dordogne is also popular with canoeists.

Croagh Patrick

County Mayo, Ireland

View: divine – as you exit, the view from the mountain appears in all its magnificent glory

Situated on the summit of sacred Croagh Patrick in the west of Ireland, this loo is a haven for walkers and pilgrims alike. And using it is certainly quite an experience – to have the chance to relieve yourself after the long climb and then be greeted by this wondrous view is absolute heaven on Earth.

This could well be the world's holiest toilet block. In AD 441, it is said that St Patrick fasted on the summit for forty days and forty nights. It was from here that he supposedly banished all snakes from Ireland – a legend steeped in religious symbolism, with the serpents representing paganism, as there were no snakes in the first place.

Today, in memory of St Patrick's fast, thousands of Catholic pilgrims climb the mountain on the last Sunday of July, known as 'Reek Sunday'. Many even climb barefoot to show penitence.

Discovering a loo on the summit is quite a relief and quite a surprise. As one pilgrim commented: 'Oh blimey, it's a toilet.'

Mount Sinai

Sinai Peninsula, Egypt

View: see the stunning mountains of Sinai through gaps in the bamboo

It might seem crazy, but the best place to see the sunrise on Mount Sinai is from inside this toilet. The early-morning light is said to flood in through the bamboo, revealing the view to those seated within. It is a once-in-a-lifetime opportunity – so uplifting that it could drive a man to poetry. This is a place to see your future, a place to have an epiphany, a place to find peace.

Mount Sinai is a popular destination with both pilgrims and tourists. In the Old Testament it is said to be where Moses was handed the Ten Commandments by God. The Bedouin even call the mountain Jabal Musa, meaning 'Moses' Mountain'. However, the actual location of the biblical Mount Sinai is still open to debate.

Climbers battle against freezing temperatures and icy winds to be at the summit for sunrise. Some come more prepared than others – tourists have even been known to climb in high-heeled shoes. It is not thought that this choice of footwear carries any particular religious significance.

Tengboche Monastery

Sagarmatha National Park, Nepal

View: a happy day – the highest point on Earth from a loo

The rare photograph on the right is one of the few images ever captured of Mount Everest as seen from a toilet. It was taken on 1 January 2000 at the Tengboche Monastery, high in the Nepalese Himalayas. What a way to start a new millennium!

Facilities may be basic – a hole in the ground above a pit and bring-your-own paper. However, any loo that has a view of the highest point on Earth has to be up there as one of the greatest and most exciting on the planet.

And like many great toilets, it invites us to pause and reflect. For example: at the dawn of the next century chances are that this view will be unchanged – still serene, peaceful, magnificent and pure. However, what state will the world that lies beneath it be in?

Tengboche Monastery is an important spiritual centre for the Sherpa people. The surrounding area is a refuge for wildlife – in keeping with the Buddhist principle of peace and compassion, no animal can be hunted or killed. The peak of Everest appears at the top left of the window.

Ryoshi Restaurant

Tirtagangga, Bali, Indonesia

View: serene – sit, relax and observe life in this tranquil Balinese village

I had travelled for over twenty-four hours to reach his loo and as I approached the restaurant Wayan came out to greet me. He smiled, gave me a hug and simply said: 'You came.' A memorable moment and a memorable loo!

Tirtagangga is a small Balinese rice-farming community. As you sit in this open-fronted hero of a toilet, watching the world go by, it is fascinating to think about the co-operative farming methods being used in the paddy fields below. For centuries Balinese farmers have worked together to try to ensure their collective survival. Individuals belong to organisations called *subaks*, which oversee the even distribution of water to all members.

The *subak* system means that water flows down the mountains and through the terraced paddy fields of Bali, even reaching the farmers at the very bottom. The Balinese have turned their mountains into level playing fields.

As well as coming to see Tirtagangga's loo with a view, it is also worth visiting the village to bathe in its holy waters, which are said to have healing and anti-ageing powers.

The Valley of Longevity

Vilcabamba, Ecuador

View: the secret of eternal youth?

It is easy to forget that the way we live can directly affect the age at which we die. It is important to stop and consider this and there is nowhere more appropriate than on this splendid wooden long-drop, located high in the Ecuadorian Andes near the village of Vilcabamba.

Meaning 'sacred valley' in the Incan Quichua dialect, Vilcabamba has become famous for the extraordinary lifespan of its population. It is said that in the 'valley of longevity' many have lived well into their hundreds – there have even been rumours of individuals living to 135.

Vilcabamba's secret has been the source of much study, discussion and debate. Various theories have been put forward to explain the incredible lifespan of the population – everything from the mineral balance of the water, to the balanced climate, to the suggestion that the people of Vilcabamba can't count!

Whatever the truth, no one has yet considered that the secret could lie in the uplifting effects of open-air loos in the region. And it is about time that this theory was given the attention it deserves.

Terminal 3

Singapore Changi Airport, Singapore

View: flight SQ2 to San Francisco, via Hong Kong, prepares for boarding

There's a buzz of excitement at the urinals between Gates B6 and B7. The toilet attendant is looking extremely proud. The new Airbus A380 has just taxied past the window.

For plane-spotters, these urinals are a dream come true – to be able to pursue a hobby while answering nature's call is a real privilege. 'The only thing better than that would have been to see Concorde's final landing from a loo,' said one spotter.

It remains to be seen whether plane-spotting from toilets takes off within the wider spotting community. However, with reports that there are loos with views in at least two other international airports, Vienna and Stockholm-Arlanda, there has to be a chance.

Terminal 3 at Singapore Changi Airport opened in January 2008. It is exciting to think that this could be the future in airport toileting. As well as offering views of planes being loaded and unloaded, taxiing to and from the runway and even taking off and landing, these urinals each feature a small painted fly in the receptacle, which helps users with their aim.

Alcatraz Guard Tower

Alcatraz Island, San Francisco Bay, California, United States

View: on the job, guards had panoramic vistas of San Francisco Bay

No wonder escape from Alcatraz was considered near impossible. Security at the notorious prison was so tight that guards could even watch for break-outs when they were using the loo.

Look carefully and you can spot a toilet in the remaining guard tower. It offered unobstructed, 360-degree views of the island and San Francisco Bay. There were once several towers on Alcatraz and, although shifts in them could be long, lonely and laborious, the loo views were out of this world.

Alcatraz housed many of America's most notorious criminals, including Al Capone. Prisoners had toilets in their cells. Some faced windows, offering a tantalising glimpse of the free world through the bars. There must have been some serious escape plotting done on those loos!

Its location amidst the freezing waters and strong currents of San Francisco Bay made 'the rock' as secure as they come. In its twenty-nine-year history (1934–1963) there were fourteen escape attempts. None were successful, although five prisoners are still unaccounted for. It is assumed that they drowned in the bay. But did they?

Livingstone Island

Victoria Falls, Zambezi River, Zambia

View: 'the smoke that thunders'

In November 1855, on one of his great African adventures, Dr David Livingstone travelled by canoe to an island in the middle of the Zambesi River and became the first European to set eyes on what they called the 'Mosi-oa-Tunya' or 'the smoke that thunders'. He had just 'discovered' Victoria Falls, which he named in honour of Queen Victoria.

Now, over 150 years later, it is possible to sit on a toilet literally metres from the edge of this magnificent waterfall and relive the very moment of Livingstone's find. It is not often that you can sit on a loo and know that you are following in the footsteps of history.

Dr Livingstone's discovery was made during a transcontinental expedition across Africa – a journey that would secure his fame. While on a later expedition to trace the source of the Nile, Livingstone lost contact with the outside world and Henry Morton Stanley was famously sent by the *New York Herald* to track him down. On doing so he is said to have let out the immortal words: 'Dr Livingstone, I presume?'

Top-Secret Tunnels

Dover Castle, Dover, United Kingdom

View: a window in the white cliffs offers views of Dover Harbour

In 1940 the view from this loo was very different – thousands of troops returning home from the beaches of Dunkirk in one of the most audacious rescue missions of all time. This loo has seen it all. Here is a loo that is part of history.

It can be found in tunnels hidden in the white cliffs beneath Dover Castle. Dug during the Napoleonic Wars and modernised as war with Hitler loomed, it was in these tunnels that Vice-Admiral Ramsay masterminded 'Operation Dynamo' – the famous Dunkirk evacuation – when 338,000 troops were saved from the jaws of the enemy to fight another day.

Winston Churchill came to Dover prior to the evacuation, although it is not known whether he visited this loo and enjoyed the view. Workers in the tunnels certainly did – it was one of the only places from which you could see the outside world.

Eight years after Dunkirk, this loo must have offered a view of the Olympic torch as it arrived in Britain for the 1948 London Olympics at Wembley – a symbol of hope after a long and bloody war.

Copeland Bird Observatory

Copeland Island, County Down, Northern Ireland

View: birds through binoculars

Visiting the loo is a great way of spending some 'alone time' – getting back in touch with yourself and what makes you happy. Therefore, in an ideal world, it ought to be possible to continue pursuing your passions from the toilet. Admittedly some hobbies are more straightforward than others – reading and knitting are clearly easier than fishing or snooker – but the principle is there.

And so bravo to the Copeland Bird Observatory! Using a traditional Irish half-door, they have devised a system that not only respects privacy and protects honour, but also allows members and visitors to the island to carry on their ornithological pursuits.

Built in 1979 and soon to be given a new stone-clad finish, you can sense the love that has gone into making this toilet what it is today. And the plumbing is ingenious – the flush uses water from a nearby well, while waste is taken away through a twenty-metre pipe down into the sea. Members claim that the lobsters in the water below the pipe are the biggest in the area. Win-win!

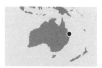

One Tree Island Research Station

The Great Barrier Reef, Australia

View: nature at its most beautiful and brutal

Many would argue that a solar-powered island in a lagoon on the Great Barrier Reef is as good as it gets. However, as good as it gets just got better. Here is a solar-powered island in a lagoon on the Great Barrier Reef that has a toilet from which you can see a colony of Black Noddy terns – mating.

For bird-watching enthusiasts this composting toilet is paradise on Earth – members of the Copeland Bird Observatory would surely relish the chance to use it. It is January and adult terns are caring for eggs and chicks. Sadly, strong winds and rain are causing their young to fall from the nests, where they are eaten by seagulls and egrets.

Black Noddy terns build their nests from dried leaves covered in their own droppings. A comforting thought as you sit on a composting toilet knowing that your droppings are about to be recycled into fertiliser.

Talk about renewable waste!

Lords

Warner Stand, Lords Cricket Ground, London, United Kingdom

View: perfectly framed – the wicket at the home of cricket

Visiting the loo while watching live sport is a dangerous game. What if you had been stuck in the toilet at the Nou Camp in 1999 as Ole Gunnar Solskjær won the European Cup for Manchester United? It is a sickening thought.

However, in the Warner Stand at Lords, gents (sorry, ladies) can visit the loo safe in the knowledge that they will not miss a single ball. Lords is the home of cricket. It is also the home of the best-placed window in the entire world.

Imagine the great sporting moments that must have been seen from these urinals! To have watched Andrew Strauss reach a century on his test debut would certainly have been quite something, while witnessing any moment of Graham Gooch's famous innings of 333 against India in 1990 would arguably have been the best toilet experience of all time.

Other stadia around the world rumoured to have loos with views are the Antigua Recreation Ground, the M.C.G. in Melbourne and New Lodge – home of Billericay Town Football Club, Essex.

'miX Lounge'

Mandalay Bay, Las Vegas, Nevada, United States

View: Interstate 15 leaves Las Vegas

When it comes to views from public loos, users of seated toilets (very often women) undoubtedly get a raw deal. It is an unacceptable imbalance in the system. While urinals are frequently found in front of windows, in the stalls you find yourself looking at your feet, reading graffiti or staring at a door.

But not in Vegas, baby! Facing a floor-to-ceiling window made from one-way glass, the functional just became phenomenal. While the 'miX Lounge' itself looks out over the Strip, its loos offer an alternative view. Sit and watch cars leaving Las Vegas on Interstate Highway 15 as it heads off south towards Los Angeles.

North to south, Interstate 15 runs from the Canadian border in Montana right through to San Diego, California. If you were to take a road trip on this highway you would not only hit Las Vegas, where you can visit one of the world's best restrooms, but would also see the 'world's tallest thermometer' (134 feet) in Baker, California (also the 'Gateway to Death Valley'), surely worth the 1,433-mile journey in itself?

Dune 45, Sossusvlei

Namib-Naukluft National Park, Namib Desert, Namibia

View: arid – one of the world's highest sand dunes in one of the oldest deserts on Earth

On the surface, this fine wooden latrine, located in the shadow of a magnificent sand dune deep in the Namib Desert, and the former England football manager Graham Taylor have absolutely nothing in common. Incredibly, however, there is a link. In 2001, a PhD student working in Namibia named a sand dune the 'G Taylor Dune' in honour of his hero.

In 1994, a Channel 4 documentary captured a team talk given by Taylor prior to a crucial game against the Netherlands, in which he spoke about the world being full of opportunities and how life's winners tended to be those who seek out and see opportunities and then take them.

England lost 2–0 and Taylor lost his job. However, his sentiments resound as you look out at this immense pile of shifting sand – constantly moving and evolving, constantly being shaped by the wind. How will the wind shape you? What opportunities will it blow your way? Will you see them and will you take them?

Close to the Salar de Uyuni

Andean High Plateau, Bolivia

View: beautifully arid landscape and a mini salt desert

Heated toilet seats, air fresheners and fancy soap are all well and good. But it is the simple things in life that have the power to make us truly happy. As one user of this stunning latrine commented: 'The toilets are quite simple, just a hole ... but the scenery is so beautiful that I wouldn't trade any golden bathroom for this one.' Amen.

It is located in the Andean High Plateau, just around the corner from the famous Salar de Uyuni – a gigantic sea of salt (the largest in the world), which stretches for thousands of square kilometres. The Salar de Uyuni was formed when a prehistoric lake dried to leave two new lakes and two huge salt flats, the larger being Uyuni.

It has been estimated that Uyuni contains ten billion tons of salt. A trip to this loo, with its considerably smaller salt plain, offers a charming glimpse of what lies ahead or reminds you that what you have just seen was not a dream.

Djankuat Glacier Research Station

Caucasus Mountains, Russia

View: a shrinking glacier and the highest mountain in Europe

Many outdoor loos without locks have novel 'engaged' systems to prevent embarrassment. And the one in place for this toilet is particularly fitting. Amazingly, occupants must leave the toilet door open to signify to others that it is being used. This system not only works, it also creates a loo with a view of the highest mountain in Europe.

The loo belongs to a research station, that lies deep within the Caucasus Mountains. The views are both significant and stunning. The last thing you see before entering is the Djankuat Glacier, one of UNESCO's reference glaciers for monitoring climate change. And inside the engaged system ensures a terrific view of Mount Elbrus.

During the Second World War, German soldiers scaled Elbrus and placed a Nazi flag on the summit, although it was later removed by the Soviets. Thinking back to this moment and with the image of the melting glacier still fresh in your mind, you are reminded of man's impact on the course of history and our ability to damage as well as save the planet on which we live.

Boston Basin High Camp

North Cascades National Park, Washington, United States

View: strong all-rounder – an uninterrupted view of Johannesburg Mountain

If you were to construct a score sheet to evaluate the standard of loos that have views, it would include the following questions:

1. Can you see the view while actually using the loo?
2. Can both men and women use it?
3. How easy is it to see the view, e.g. is a head swivel necessary?
4. How good is the view?
5. How interesting and/or thought-provoking is the view?
6. Is the view unobstructed? (a wall, tree, fence or bush might block the line of sight)
7. How user-friendly is the loo?
8. What is the overall impact on the user?

While the answers to some questions are of course subjective, few would disagree that the Boston Basin loo scores well in almost every area. A spectacular, unspoiled, uninterrupted, sweeping vista, lies directly in front of you while seated – and for added entertainment it is even located near a colony of marmots!

The Boston Basin privy – setting the standard for all-round excellence in loo viewing.

Spider Rock

Canyon de Chelly, Chinle, Arizona, United States

View: Spider Rock rises from the floor of this sacred Navajo canyon

It had been a long hike in baking temperatures from the rim down to the canyon floor. And suddenly there it was – awesome, beautiful and magnificent – at the base of an 800-foot sandstone spire, the best-placed family toilet on the planet.

Humans have lived in the Canyon de Chelly (pronounced 'de shay') for thousands of years. The Native American Navajo people entered the canyon in around 1700. And many still live here in their spiritual home today. In the summer, Navajo families move into the canyon to farm their lands and raise sheep, living in traditional-style homes, called hogans.

Although the canyon feels peaceful today, this has not always been the case. Perhaps most famously, in 1864 US forces stormed the canyon and killed or captured most of the Navajo within it. Prisoners were forced to walk for over three hundred miles to Fort Sumner – known as the 'Long Walk' – where they faced incarceration for the next four years before being allowed to return home.

Mount Whitney

Sierra Nevada, California, United States

View: absolute freedom – sit and take in the triumphant view from the summit loo

Infamous amongst the climbing community for many years, reports suggest that this toilet is sadly now no more. Where this proud, bald-headed eagle of a loo once stood, now sit only rocks. It may be gone but it will not be forgotten.

Exposed to the elements and boasting an awe-inspiring, panoramic view, this loo took toileting to a whole new level. It was a latrine with one hell of an attitude – a pumped-up, adrenalin-fuelled, roller-coaster ride of a loo.

In just one single hour screams of 'awesome', 'I love being me' and 'man, that's good' were all heard coming from the direction of this loo. It was a toilet that made you feel free. It was a toilet that made you want to stand up and shout, 'God bless America!'

At over 14,500 feet, the summit of Mount Whitney is the highest point in the contiguous United States. Amazingly, just a few hours east of this giant mountain is the lowest point in North America, eighty-six metres below sea level, at Death Valley.

Tasman Saddle Hut

Tasman Glacier, South Island, New Zealand

View: a loo from above – and on the edge

We have seen that it is possible to spot planes from toilets. However few would have believed that it is also possible to spot toilets from planes.

Taken in 1990 from high above New Zealand's Tasman Glacier, this rare archive photograph proves that it can be done. Although the loo has since been upgraded, this still stands as one of the few images ever captured of a loo from the air.

It makes you want more. Perhaps it is time for loo-spotting pleasure flights – giving the general public the opportunity to see some of the world's most remote, out-there and on-the-edge toilets. You heard it here first.

Where will the relationship between loos and planes end? There have even been reports that some airlines have windows in their upper-class toilets, theoretically making it possible to spot a loo on the ground from a loo in a plane!

Now there is a mile-high club you want to be a part of.

Mount McKinley

Denali National Park, Alaska, United States

View: a 'great one' – Mount Foraker from 14,200 feet

While observing loos from planes clearly has a lot of potential as a tourist enterprise, nothing beats getting out into the wilderness yourself and experiencing them first-hand. Only in freezing temperatures, with the wind lashing at your cheeks, can you truly appreciate the wondrous sense of escape that loos with views can provide. 'Adventure toileting' – it ought to be an Olympic sport.

This image was captured in May 2006 on a successful expedition to the summit of Mount McKinley. At 20,320 feet, McKinley is the highest mountain in North America. Although the peak is nearer sea level, the mountain's rise of 18,000 feet from base to peak is far greater than that of Mount Everest.

Many prefer to call Mount McKinley by its original name, Denali, which means 'great one' in the native Athapaskan language. Denali was renamed after William McKinley in 1896, shortly before he became the twenty-fifth president of the United States. President McKinley was assassinated by an anarchist in 1901 and replaced by number twenty-six, Theodore Roosevelt.

The Station Inn

Ribblehead, North Yorkshire Dales, United Kingdom

View: the famous Ribblehead Viaduct – a dream come true for trainspotters

If there was a competition for Britain's best view from a pub urinal, the left-hand installation at the Station Inn would be odds-on favourite. With a clear view of a magnificent twenty-four-arch railway viaduct, this is pub toileting at its most exhilarating.

The Ribblehead Viaduct is the iconic image of the Settle–Carlisle Railway. It was constructed in the early 1870s – part of the nineteenth-century railway boom, which transformed the face of Britain and the world.

Thousands of 'navvies', who built the viaduct largely by hand, lived in shanty towns on the moor during the years of construction. Many workers and members of their families were killed in industrial accidents and smallpox epidemics. Over 200 are buried in a nearby churchyard.

Using the urinal while a train is crossing the viaduct can be the cause of tremendous excitement at the inn. As railway enthusiast Lawrence Knowles exclaimed: 'Lads, I've just seen the 15.23 to Leeds heading over the viaduct while I was peeing. What a rush!'

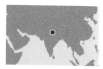

Kosi Kalan Railway Station, Platform 2

Kosi Kalan, Uttar Pradesh, India

View: passengers on platform 1 await the arrival of the Agra-Delhi Express

If they have not been already, Ribblehead and the Indian town of Kosi Kalan ought to be twinned. Although at first glance they have absolutely nothing in common, they share a very special bond – united by the fact that they both have a loo from which you can spot trains.

And there are certainly plenty to spot in India. The country's railway system is one of the largest in the world, employing something like 1.6 million people. At the time that the Ribblehead Viaduct was being finished in the 1870s, the railways were already well developed in the British Indian Empire, covering some 9,000 miles by 1880.

Another railway station said to have a loo with a view is at Fishhoek on the Cape Peninsula in South Africa. During the mating and calving season (July–November), it is said to be possible to see Southern Right Whales while seated. Could it actually get any better?

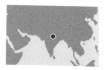

The Maharaja Suite

Sheesh Mahal Palace, Orchha, India

View: standing – the ruins of an Indian kingdom; sitting – a pair of Indian parakeets

Very few indoor toilets have views while seated *and* standing, which makes this find so exciting. Located in the 'Maharaja Suite' of a government-run hotel in a former Indian palace, this loo offers a double whammy of pleasure. Here is a throne fit for a king.

The view while standing takes you back to the time of the Bundela kings, who ruled from Orchha between the sixteenth and eighteenth centuries. You stand and picture lavish royal living – camel and elephant houses, ornate gardens, dancing girls, concubines, bathing houses and hunting expeditions into the forest beyond.

While seated you may see a pair of green Indian ring-necked parakeets, which perch on a ledge just outside the window. The chemistry between these lovebirds is electric, making this the perfect place for some loo-based heart-searching.

The Sheesh Mahal sits next to the Jahangir Mahal, a magnificent palace built by the Bundela King Bir Singh Deo to commemorate the visit of the Moghul Emperor Jahangir. It was Jahangir's son, Shah Jahan, who built the famous Taj Mahal in Agra.

Mount Ruapehu

Tongariro National Park, North Island, New Zealand

View: from Hollywood to dunnywood, Mount Ngauruhoe hovers gracefully above the clouds

Unless you are a particularly twisted type of celebrity stalker it is not every day that you see a major film star while visiting a loo. However, this photograph – captured on New Zealand's Mount Ruapehu – proves that it can be done by the general public without breaking the law.

And there she is. Sitting in the distance, her cone elegantly raised above the clouds – Mount Ngauruhoe, a.k.a. the evil Mount Doom in Peter Jackson's celebrated *Lord of the Rings* trilogy.

When not appearing as the home of the 'fires of Mordor' in feature films, Mount Ngauruhoe spends its time as an active volcano in Tongariro National Park on the North Island of New Zealand. The park is the oldest National Park in New Zealand.

Eyewitness accounts suggest that there is no view from inside this loo – just a door. However, the general splendour of its location makes it a top loo nonetheless.

Mackinnon Pass

Milford Track, South Island, New Zealand

View: dunnytastic – stand proud and see Clinton Canyon open before your eyes

Even Shakespeare was into toilets. It has been argued that in *As You Like It* the great man named one of his characters, the melancholy Jaques, after a medieval word for toilet, 'jakes'. It is good to know that toilet humour was alive and well at the Globe.

And as Jaques famously says in Act 2, Scene 7: 'All the world's a stage'. Whether Shakespeare meant this line to apply to toilets is doubtful. Nevertheless, this dramatic loo with a view, located on the Milford Track in New Zealand, does have a very theatrical quality.

From backstage, inside the toilet, you catch a glimpse of the view through a window in the door. And then as you exit you make your entrance onto the great platform. The valley opens before you like a pair of curtains. And there it is – the view.

But like a play, the moment does not last for ever. As Jaques says, we all have our exits and our entrances. You take in the view, then take your cue and go on your way.

Jin Mao Building

Grand Hyatt Hotel, Pudong, Shanghai, China

View: from the 56th floor, Shanghai's Oriental Pearl Tower and the Huangpu River

To see truly world-famous sights while using a loo is not always easy. Sometimes it can take both ruthlessness and flexibility. And here is the perfect example. All four of the urinals in this splendid restroom easily offer a view of Shanghai's financial district, Pudong. However, to catch a glimpse of the famous Oriental Pearl Tower takes a little extra commitment to the cause.

First, it is necessary to secure the urinal nearest the window, furthest right. Then, to see the view in all its glory requires a daring 'lean back, neck swivel' manoeuvre. It has been tried and can be done (at your own risk of course).

As well as the spectacular views and location in the super-high eighty-eight-storey Jin Mao Building, the other great thing about these urinals is the divider between the loo and the window, fifty-six floors up, to protect your modesty from the outside world.

Now that is the definition of class.

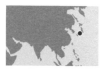

Mumin Papa Café

Akashi, Hyogo Prefecture, Japan

View: incredibly, this toilet has been built into an aquarium

Many of the world's most extraordinary toilet experiences lie tantalisingly out of reach. You hear the rumours and read about sightings, but to see them with your own eyes would take years of planning, as well as a degree of luck. Sadly, spotting the Northern Lights, observing whales mating, seeing a rainbow over Machu Picchu and viewing the Earth from space have, thus far, remained elusive.

However, the good news is that in the ladies' loo at the Mumin Papa Café the experience of toileting underwater (while surrounded by a variety of marine animalia) is now perfectly possible.

All too often, women get the short straw when it comes to views from loos. This loo helps to redress the balance. Sit, relax and feel like a mermaid being cradled in the gentle arms of the goddess of the sea.

But can you relax? The loo was recently featured on Japanese television, where the owner explained that a sea turtle living in the aquarium is male and likes to stare at the ladies sitting on the loo!

Cloud Forest

Horton Plains National Park, Sri Lanka

View: 'tree-mendous' – here is a loo situated in the middle of a tropical forest

Trying to find loos with views is like a sickness – an obsession. You spend your entire life on the lookout. You can't go anywhere without popping into the loo for a quick look. You also spend much of your life feeling disappointed – if you visit somewhere really special or see a beautiful view you just end up wishing that there was a toilet there.

Finding loos with views is a little bit like finding love. Just when you least expect it, completely out of the blue they turn up in the most unlikely places. Like here – hidden deep within a tropical Sri Lankan cloud forest.

Cloud forests are a special type of rainforest, found at relatively high altitudes. You can normally spot a cloud forest by the fact that it is covered in cloud.

The cloud certainly makes it less easy to spot loos with views. But occasionally they find you, appearing out of the mist to rock your world.

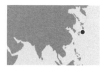

Asahi Beer Headquarters, Top Floor Bar

Asakusa, Tokyo, Japan

View: the Sumida River flows through Tokyo on its way to Tokyo Bay

Standing at this top-notch urinal and looking out at modern-day Tokyo – now a huge, densely populated metropolis – it is hard to believe that the city began life as a small fishing village called Edo.

In the late 1500s, at a time when samurai warriors fought on the battlefields of Japan, the head of a powerful clan, Tokugawa Ieyasu, moved his base to Edo. Tokugawa was appointed shogun in AD 1603 and established a dynasty that ruled Japan for over 250 years, while Edo grew into a city of over one million inhabitants.

Officially at least Kyoto remained the capital. But when imperial power was restored to Japan in 1868 (after centuries of merely symbolic leadership) the emperor moved to Edo, which was renamed Tokyo, meaning 'eastern capital'. It was the start of Japan's modern history.

Just in case it ever comes up in a pub quiz over a pint of beer!

Mequat Mariam

Meket Plateau, Ethiopian Highlands, Ethiopia

View: the 'Roof of Africa'

Walking at almost 3,000 metres above sea level, the trek takes you across the Meket Plateau to a spectacular escarpment and your home for the night - the thatched *tukuls* of Mequat Mariam. And (would you believe it?) one of them – the open-fronted *tukul* nearest the camera – happens to house one of the finest loos with a view in all of Africa.

Your hosts at Mequat Mariam work in partnership with an organisation called 'Tourism in Ethiopia for Sustainable Future Alternatives' (TESFA), a non-profit-making NGO, which helps local communities in the Ethiopian Highlands build services for tourists. Four villages now host tourists on the Meket Plateau and more are developing facilities, including, of course, loos with views.

Sitting in this magnificent *tukul*, watching birds soaring in the skies above and knowing that your business is helping communities to develop in one of the world's poorest countries, offers a sense of well-being that is not easy to find in the world today. This is the perfect way to start or end your day. This is the perfect way to see the world.

Felix Bar

Peninsula Hotel, Kowloon, Hong Kong

View: classic loo-based tourism – see Hong Kong Harbour and Island from the ladies' restroom

It was a tough call deciding whether to feature the ladies' or the gents' at the Felix. While the men's is well known for its urinal views of Kowloon (giving it a much higher 'view from the actual loo' rating), the fact that ladies can powder their noses while looking at one of the world's most iconic views makes this a female victory.

Hong Kong Harbour is also known as Victoria Harbour – after Her Royal Highness, who was on the throne when Britain took control of Hong Kong in the 1840s. Also named after Queen Victoria are Lake Victoria in East Africa, Victoria Falls, the Victoria sponge cake and Victoria Park, home of Hartlepool United Football Club.

This is not the only Hong Kong-based loo to appear in a book. Rumour has it that a loo with a view at the former premises of the Foreign Correspondents' Club of Hong Kong, Sutherland House, was featured in the John le Carré spy thriller *The Honourable Schoolboy*.

Kalamu Tented Camp

The Banks of the South Luangwa River, Zambia

View: wallowing hippopotami

We have seen that loos with views allow us to sightsee from the toilet. However, another popular tourist pursuit, also perfectly possible from loos, is big-game spotting. The safari parks of Africa are a gold mine for loos with views. Elephant, hippo, crocodile – numerous sightings have been recorded. Put down the morning paper – this is the only way to start the day.

To see all of the 'big five' (lion, elephant, buffalo, rhino and leopard) or to see a kill from the loo is incredibly rare, incredibly difficult and takes incredible dedication – or incredible bowel trouble.

But there is plenty to contemplate as you wait: the great 'circle of life', as discussed in Disney's *The Lion King*; how 'survival of the fittest' theories became ingrained into Fascist ideas about the survival of nations with catastrophic effects; or the thought that we look at animals going to the loo all the time and think nothing of it, but looking at animals while we go to the loo somehow feels a bit surreal!

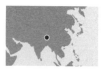

Samye Monastery

Shannan, Tibet

View: from this communal, triple toilet (sadly only two loos are in view here), a shrine at the oldest monastery in Tibet

You could devote an entire book to communal toileting. From Roman soldiers to farmers in the Australian outback to Buddhist monks, going 'en masse' is not only a part of human history, it is also common practice in a number of cultures today.

Even in Britain, a country known for its prudish sensibilities, it was not so long ago that children grew up on two-seater toilets in their back gardens. Rare 'three-seaters' have even been discovered.

Collective toileting, while perhaps initially off-putting, is good for the soul – solid, character-building stuff. What conversations must have been had and what relationships must have been forged. Has there ever been a marriage proposal?

Rising divorce rates, a breakdown in family values and a lack of community are all big issues in the modern world. But perhaps the answer is staring us right in the face? Perhaps the answer is communal toilets?

Galata Tower

Galata, Istanbul, Turkey

View: intercontinental toileting – from Europe into Asia, while seated

There are only a handful of places on Earth where it is possible to sit on a loo and see into another continent. With views across the Bosporus Strait into Asia, this fine throne, located high in Istanbul's Galata Tower, is one of them. The window is made of frosted glass, but opens to create a quite magnificent loo with a view. 'Breezy but breathtaking,' commented one American tourist.

Throughout its history, Istanbul has been a place of great strategic and commercial importance – the centre of empires. For centuries the city was known as Constantinople after the Roman Emperor Constantine, who declared it the capital of the Roman Empire in the fourth century.

The Galata Tower was built in 1348. In the seventeenth century, when Istanbul was under Ottoman control, it is said that an early aviator called Hezarfen Ahmet Çelebi jumped from the top of the tower and glided with artificial wings across the Bosporus. Had this toilet existed at the time, he may have wished to use it before making his historic leap.

St Helen's Oratory

Upstairs Bathroom, Cape Cottage, Cornwall,
United Kingdom
View: the site of an ancient Christian chapel and wild Atlantic
coastline

And so here is where the journey began – a freckly-faced,
floppy-haired young lad sits on a loo and sees a view. Cows
were grazing, waves were crashing against the rocks and the
sun was shining. What a moment and what a loo.

The chapel, known as St Helen's Oratory, may date back to
around the fifth century. It is certainly likely to have been built
after Emperor Constantine's famous conversion in AD 312,
which transformed Christianity into an official religion within
the Roman Empire. Constantine's conversion changed the
course of human history – little did he know that centuries
later it would also create this fantastic loo view.

Well-placed windows in bathrooms can take us to places we
never dreamed we would go and into worlds that we never
thought we would visit. Everyone should have access to a loo
with a view – they change lives.

Incredibly, a family in the west of England are currently
considering moving their toilet three feet to the right to give
it a view of the largest church cockerel in Europe! Now that's
the spirit.

Acknowledgements

I would like to thank everyone who has helped to make this book possible. Alone, my search would surely have been futile.

For their support and patience: my family; Hattie Wood; Anna and Matt Cardy; Joe Burns; Claudia Shaffer; Libby Mourant and Jon Hawkins.

To everyone who has sent me or let me include their wonderful photographs.

To the team at Virgin Books, especially Ed Faulkner and Davina Russell.

To those who have shared their loo-view experiences with me, especially Irene Cahill and Ken Levan.

To English Heritage at Dover Castle; the legendary Wayan; the Copeland Bird Observatory; One Tree Island Research Station; TESFA; the Department of Conservation, New Zealand and the US National Park Service. To Howard Smith; Miyuki Kogi; Tom Henson; Kimberly Deni; Brendan Maguire; Brian McKeon; Chiaki Yamauchi; Isabel Ollivier; John Cantwell; Mike Fletcher; the Samli Family; Lesley Bellus; and many more.

But most of all, thanks to the loos – I couldn't have done it without you guys…

Photo Credits

Pages 2 and 3 © Bryan Long; 6 © Arman Rin, Jr; 7 © David Gómez-Rosado and Lorena Fernández-Fernández, 2006; 8 © John Taggart, 9 © Cedric Babled; 12, 13, 66, 67 © Chris Belsten; 14 © Wendy Cue; 15 © Anna Maria S. Jorgensen; 18 and 19 © Nathan Thadani; 24 © Josh & Amber Johnson; 25 © Jocelyn King; 26, 27, 52, 53 © Anna Cardy; 28 and 29 © Neville McKee; 30 and 31 © Jennifer Reiffel; 36 and 37 © Hannah Woodthorpe; 38 and 39 © Maxime Renaudin; 40 and 41 © Chris R Stokes; vii, 42 and 43 © Adam Russell; 46 and 47 © Larry Mah; 48 and 49 © Kim Ollivier; 50 and 51 © Pat Baumann; 58 and 59 © David Briese; 60 and 61© Andrew Wooster; 64 and 65 © Emerald Huang; 70 © Susan Grant; 71 © Mark Chapman; 72 and 73 © Ryan Wong; 74 © Caroline Culbert, courtesy of Wilderness Safaris, 75 © Dana Allen, courtesy of Wilderness Safaris; 76 and 77 © Diana and Bart-Willem van Leeuwen; xi, xii, 1, 4, 5, 10, 11, 16, 17, 20, 21, 22, 23, 32, 33, 34, 35, 44, 45, 54, 55, 56, 57, 62, 63, 68, 69, 78, 79, 80, 81 © Luke Barclay; 86 © Burt Rosen

The Loo List

A Loo with a View: The Search Continues...

I thought I had found the definitive list of loos with views, but then I realised that my search had only just begun. If you have come across or perhaps even own a loo with a view, I would love to hear from you: loos@looswithviews.com